D0835486

muffin
magic

Susannah Blake

Photography by Yuki Sugiyura

PAVILION

First published in the United Kingdom in 2009 by
Pavilion Books
Old West London Magistrates Court
10 Southcombe Street
London, W14 0RA

An imprint of Anova Books Company Ltd

Design and layout © Pavilion, 2009
Text © Susannah Blake, 2009
Photography © Yuki Sugiyura, 2009, except page 12 © cakeadoodledo.co.uk

The moral right of the author has been asserted.

All rights reserved. No part of this publication may be reproduced, stored in
a retrieval system, or transmitted in any form or by any means electronic,
mechanical, photocopying, recording or otherwise, without the prior written
permission of the copyright owner.

Commissioning editor: Emily Preece-Morrison
Designer: Anna Pow
Cover designer: Georgina Hewitt
Production: Rebekah Cheyne
Home economist: Valerie Berry
Stylist: Wei Tang
Photographer: Yuki Sugiyura
Case illustration: Lotte Oldfield
Copy editor: Barbara Dixon
Indexer: Patricia Hymans

ISBN 978-1-862058-48-4

A CIP catalogue record for this book is available from the British Library.

10 9 8 7 6 5 4 3 2 1

Reproduction by Dot Gradations, United Kingdom
Printed and bound by SNP Leefung Printers Ltd, China

www.anovabooks.com

Contents

Introduction 5

Ingredients 8

Kitchen basics 10

Happy hens, happy eggs 12

1 Faff-free 14

2 Kiddie-friendly 32

3 Adults only 58

4 Savoury 76

5 Seasonal 94

Index 110

Acknowledgements 112

Introduction

Marvellous, marvellous muffins! Versatile, easy-to-make and with that indisputable, indefinable feel-good factor – they're just utterly irresistible. And the fabulous thing about muffins is that they really are perfect for every occasion...

* Breakfast booster
* Mid-morning snack
* Lunchbox luxury
* Post-lunch treat
* Afternoon tea
* Post-supper sweetie
* Midnight munchie
* Naughty nibble
* Savoury something
* Gorgeous gift

Muffins tick every box when it comes to finding a certain something to fill the gap. They seem to lift the spirits, put a smile on your face and just make you feel better about life. They should be light and fluffy, still warm from the oven (my preference), crumbly and golden (or dark brown if you're going down the choccy route), and so good that you'll probably want to squeeze a second one into your mouth when no one's looking!

Sometimes I do find myself pondering over what all the fuss about muffins is. I mean, obviously they taste good – but they're just so easy to make. Measure, stir, dollop, bake – that's all there is to it. There's no particular 'magic' about them – unless, of course, the magic is that they're so simple, and so good ... almost a culinary miracle in the making?

Muffins come in such myriad shapes, sizes, flavours and colours that sometimes you need to think long and hard about where your muffin will best fit. What time? What occasion? Maybe even how to serve it?

A simple fruity muffin seems to naturally fit the breakfast criteria. Add some fruit and it's virtually a health product (kind of) and if the recipe's easy, you might actually feel up to tackling it when you've just crawled out of bed. The 'simple, fruity' criteria probably make the muffins kiddie-friendly as well – not too full of naughty ingredients, and easy enough that you can still follow the recipe while a herd of marauding under-fives swarm around your feet.

When it comes to chocolate or frosted muffins, I like to think this elevates a muffin into the treat category. Now, you can have treats any time of day and, to be honest, any day of the week, but there's something about the extra sugar and yumminess that chocolate and frosting introduce that transforms these types of muffins into more of an indulgence for the soul, one of those goodies that nurtures your spirit and makes you feel better about life.

And then, of course, there's that old chestnut – the savoury muffin. Lots of people forget about these ... and that's a crime! Savoury muffins are marvellous and good for every category: healthy breakfast food, feel-good factor, snack, or accompaniment to a meal.

And what about muffins for special occasions? Well, any muffin worth its salt is good for a special occasion. But if in doubt – go for a muffin that fulfils the 'treat' criteria and you won't go far wrong.

There's only one drawback about muffins, although not everyone will consider it so. They're much, much better when they're freshly made, so you really, honestly do have to eat them on the day you make them. Personally, I'm a little bit brutal about these things – muffins are an indulgence, and where's the indulgent luxury in something that's not at its absolute best? So go on, dig in and gobble them up as quickly as you can!

The secret to perfect, perfect muffins

I'd like to pretend there's a huge amount of skill and talent involved in baking a batch of golden-brown, sweetly scented muffins – but I'm afraid I'd be lying. They are so unbelievably easy-peasy to make, pretty much anyone can do it – even self-professed failures in the kitchen. But there are a few secrets to making really light fluffy muffins (the third of which may well appeal directly to the more slapdash cooks among us).

Number 1: To make a sweeping generalisation – combine your dry ingredients, combine your wet ingredients, put the two together and bingo: 12 muffins!

But before you get to this stage, there's a golden rule...

Number 2: Even if this seems like a faff, do it anyway! Sift all your dry ingredients together before you add the wet ingredients. You want your flour, sugar, cocoa, etc. to be as light as air, filling your mixing bowl in soft drifts like freshly fallen snow.

Number 3: Once you add the wet ingredients, don't over-mix! The temptation will be to give the batter a good old beating to make sure you've got a lovely smooth mixture. But this is wrong, wrong, wrong. Give it a gentle, brief stir – just enough to combine the ingredients, but no more than that. The average muffin mixture will still look a bit lumpy and chunky, and if you've still got a few streaks of flour – don't worry about it. Just scoop up big spoonfuls of the mixture, dollop them into the cases, then bung the tray in the oven. Twenty minutes later you'll be in heaven and wondering why you don't make these gorgeous creations every morning.

And if you don't follow this advice? Well, they'll still be edible, but your muffins won't have that fabulously fluffy texture that all the best muffins should have. They'll be a little tough, a little bit more solid than you'd like. So take my advice and always give your muffins the quick 1-2-3 treatment.

Ingredients

So now you know *how* to make your muffins, but what do you put in them? Well, that's simple: nice things. And when I say 'nice', I don't just mean tasty, I mean things that make you feel good. I like my treats to be guilt-free – so choose eggs from free-range chickens, milk and butter from happy cows, coffee and chocolate that's been fairly traded. You know what I'm talking about. For full muffin enjoyment, nobody (and nothing) should have suffered. (Except possibly your mouth, if you're too eager to let your muffins cool down before taking a big, fat, greedy gobble ... or your waistline, if you can't stop at just one...)

So once you've thought about where your ingredients come from, you might wonder what they are. Well, the main players are flour, baking powder (because you want your muffins to be *really* light and fluffy), eggs, milk and butter. There are, of course, variations such as oil or yogurt or sour cream or buttermilk, but I'm talking about your real basics here. When you've got the basics, then you can start adding the flavourings: sugar and spice, summer berries, nutty nuts, cheeky chocolate, dried fruit... Once you get going, you'll find the list is pretty much never-ending. Vanilla? Lemon? Orange? Coffee? These flavours were just made for making muffins.

The good thing about muffins is that although they're great just as they are – still warm and tender and crumbly from the oven – they're even better topped. The usual suspects work brilliantly: flavoured butters and sweet buttercreams, cream cheese frostings, simple glacé icings, melted chocolate, plain old cream cheese, or mascarpone. The list goes on and on – and it's oh-so-good! Indulge yourself, why don't you, and go mad with smearing, swirling, spreading and sprinkling.

Allergy-free

If you suffer from food allergies or intolerance, muffin baking and eating can get a bit tricky. If it's just nuts or soya or yeast or chocolate you're trying to avoid, there are plenty of recipes for you to choose, which means the door's still open if you want to go mad for muffins without worrying about the after-effects.

However, if you're avoiding gluten, dairy products, or eggs, you're in for a tougher time. Not to put too fine a point on it, flour, butter, milk and eggs are the bedrock of your average muffin. And they make them taste good.

But don't worry, hope is not lost. You can still make fabulously fun, funky muffins without resorting to those ingredients. There are loads of muffins that can be made with oil in place of melted butter, and there are lots of dairy-free milks – from soya milk to almond milk to oat milk. As for gluten, there are various flours you can use, potato, rice, corn and soya being my favourites. When it comes to eggs, although more of a challenge, it *is* still possible to make a gorgeous muffin without them. I've made sure there's a good choice of muffins that are free of these ingredients, so even the most severe allergics among us can still indulge themselves.

For dairy-free muffins, try: Muesli Morning Muffins on page 30, Peanut Butter and Choc Chip Cheekies on page 36 (with the ingredient tweaks suggested in the intro), Figgy Oatmeal Muffins on page 51, Cool and Creamy Carrot Cake on page 71, Ole South Chilli Cornmeal Muffins on page 89, or Easter Muffins on page 96

For gluten-free muffins, try: Date and Ginger Honeys on page 26, Luscious Lemon and Raspberry Muffins on page 68, or Easter Muffins on page 96.

For egg-free muffins, try: Blueberry Bliss on page 21.

Kitchen basics

In terms of kitchen equipment, you don't need much to bake a muffin (or twelve). Just an oven, some scales, a measuring jug, some measuring spoons, a big bowl and a wooden spoon for mixing, a sieve for sifting, maybe a saucepan for melting or warming, possibly a fork for whisking up those liquid ingredients. And, of course, a muffin pan. Don't kid yourself, this is the one essential you absolutely cannot do without, but it's an investment you won't regret.

How big is your muffin?

Now, *that* is the sixty million dollar question. We've established that you need a muffin pan and, personally, I like to line mine with pretty paper cases. You *can* just grease the cups of the muffin pan, but the finished muffins look so much more appealing in paper cases – and it'll make your washing up so much easier, plus there are the benefits of cases for muffin transportation should you wish to consume muffins outside the home. You can get plain old white muffin papers in every supermarket, and many stock pretty patterned ones as well. But it's worth having a search in kitchen shops, too, because it's here that you'll find the best selection of colours and patterns to add a little bit of flair to your muffin making.

But what size of pan and papers? Muffin pans and cases come in a mind-boggling array of sizes and it would be fair to wonder – which ones should I use? As a general rule, I've used a medium-sized muffin pan for the recipes in this book. Which means the batter quantities are enough for twelve fantastic muffins. So, should you wish to use a muffin pan with larger cups, that's absolutely fine. You'll just find that you

end up with fewer muffins, but they'll be a whole lot bigger – and you may need to bake them for a minute or two longer.

A few of the recipes in this book use a mini muffin pan, so you get lots of little diddy muffins. But again, if you want to use one of the basic muffin mixtures and cook it in a mini muffin pan – go ahead and just reduce the cooking time accordingly. (You'll also need to halve the recipe quantities – unless you want to make a gazillion muffins!)

You can also find muffin pans in funky shapes. My favourite is the heart-shaped muffin pan, which will produce the most gorgeously cute heart-shaped muffins imaginable. But if you're thinking you'll only use a heart-shaped muffin pan once a year so it's not worth the investment – think again! Obviously there's Valentine's Day, but then your lover will adore you for making them heart-shaped muffins any day of the year; a batch for your mother on Mother's Day will make her crumple with pleasure; a plateful for the girls just because they're girls... You see, the possibilities are endless!

Oven tips

Now it may seem obvious, but try to use your common sense when you're baking. Every oven is different and has its own special foibles. Some ovens cook slightly quicker, some slightly slower. Some ovens have 'hot patches' so you'll need to turn the tray to prevent half your muffins browning more than the other half. Once you've baked one or two recipes from this book, you might find you always have to cook your muffins for a minute more or a minute less. These recipes are all tested to perfection – but they've obviously been tested in my oven, not yours, so please, please let common sense prevail.

Happy hens, happy eggs

Now I know I've already talked about using 'nice' ingredients, but I feel the need to harp on a little bit more on the issue of eggs. Although you *can* make muffins without eggs, the vast majority of muffin recipes are going to call for at least one egg, if not two. And if you're taking this book seriously, you're going to be trying out a lot of muffin recipes. Multiply that by one or two eggs for every batch of muffins you bake – and you will be buying a whole lot of eggs before your muffin days are over.

When it comes to choosing eggs, it's really a no-brainer. They need to be free-range. The hens that laid the eggs should have been free to roam around outside, pecking about, looking for food, deciding what they fancy and snapping it up. They should have had enough space to open up their wings and have a good flap, and the opportunity of a hedge to scuttle under should the mood take them. They just need the basics, just like *you* expect the basics.

What they should not have been subjected to is being crammed into a cage that's not even big enough to turn around in, then condemned to a life of eating and laying, eating and laying. And, of course, once their production drops and they're past their prime, they should still be valued, they shouldn't just be discarded because it's taking them more than a day to produce an egg. I'm talking about battery farming here – it's not very nice, so please do avoid the eggs produced from battery-farmed hens because you're not helping anyone ... least of all the hens.

You can do your bit by purchasing only free-range eggs and products that use free-range eggs (that is egg sandwiches, cakes, biscuits, mayonnaise, quiches, pasta...), and this book does a little bit more. For every copy sold, a donation is made to the Battery Hen Welfare Trust (BHWT). This wonderful organisation, which works in a constructive and positive way with the industry and those farmers producing battery-farmed eggs, aims to promote and ensure a happier, better life for the 20 million battery hens currently in cages. The BHWT's goal is to inspire us, the public, to do all we possibly can to achieve a better future for these hens – whether it's through our supermarket shopping, or by us adopting a battery hen (or six, see below) – and thus help farmers to consider and facilitate the options for change to produce and keep happier hens. Check out BHWT's website at *www.bhwt.org.uk* to find out more about what you can do to live in a world of happier, cluckier hens.

Raising your own

For the really hardened chicken welfarer, there's another exciting option. If you've got space and time, and your council allows the raising of hens in your area, you can adopt a hen from the BHWT and reap the reward not only of freshly laid eggs, produced with the aid of your good self, but also the pleasure of transforming a pale and balding bird that's not even quite sure how to peck or flap into a pecking, clucking, flapping, feathery brown hen that's as happy as any hen can be. And hens really do make surprisingly good pets – they're friendly, cheeky and, best of all, pretty low-maintenance. So check out hen houses and spacious runs and the options for adopting, and enjoy your egg-laying hens in the way they should be enjoyed ... through the medium of the muffin!

Faff-free

1

These muffins are exactly what they say on the label: free of faff. Even the most slapdash, un-kitchen-friendly cook would struggle to get these babies wrong. They use the minimum of ingredients, require the minimum of skill and culinary flair, and you can enjoy them straight from the oven – no faffing around with fancy frostings or frills (lovely as they are). The ones that do have a cheeky topping or two are like the main muffin recipes – just unbelievably easy and almost impossible to get wrong. (But if a frosting seems like just too much effort, you can always leave it off. Just whip the muffins out of the oven, dust them down with a bit of icing sugar and eat them as soon as you possibly can.)

Another bonus about these recipes is that because they're faff-free they're the perfect choice for unexpected guests, or when you require an indulgent breakfast. If you're planning ahead in the breakfast department, try to remember to measure out the ingredients the night before so you can just get up, bung the oven on, throw the ingredients together and lo ... a batch of warm, golden muffins fit for a king (or queen)!

Coconut-lime muffins

For the truly faff-free muffin, you can serve these little beauties just as they are, still warm from the oven. But for the ultimate limey, coconutty, creamy experience, go the whole mile and serve them with lashings of cream cheese frosting and piles of snowy-white coconut shavings.

✳ Makes 12

300 g/10 oz/2 cups self-raising flour
1 tsp baking powder
150 g/5 oz/⅔ cup caster sugar
1 egg, beaten
200 ml/7 fl oz/generous ¾ cup coconut milk
grated zest of 2 limes
100 ml/3½ fl oz/scant ½ cup sunflower oil
50 g/1¾ oz/½ cup desiccated coconut

To decorate
150 g/5 oz cream cheese
50 g/1¾ oz/⅓ cup icing sugar
2 tsp lime juice
coconut shavings, for sprinkling

Preheat the oven to 200°C/400°F/Gas 6. Grease or line a 12-hole muffin pan.

Combine the flour, baking powder and caster sugar and sift into a large bowl.

In a separate bowl or jug, combine the egg, coconut milk, lime zest and juice, oil and desiccated coconut, then pour into the dry ingredients. Stir together until just combined, then spoon big dollops of the mixture into the prepared muffin pan.

Bake for about 20 minutes until risen and golden. Leave to cool in the pan for a couple of minutes, then transfer to a wire rack to cool.

To serve, beat together the cream cheese, icing sugar and lime juice until smooth and creamy. Swirl on top of the muffins and sprinkle with coconut shavings.

Apple muffins with cinnamon butter

Throw together a batch of these comforting muffins and find your kitchen filled with the sweet smell of cinnamon. For a faff-free but to-die-for twist, serve them still warm, broken open and smeared with melting cinnamon butter.

✻ Makes 12

300 g/10 oz/2 cups self-raising
  flour
½ tsp bicarbonate of soda
1 tsp ground cinnamon
2 eggs, beaten
75 ml/3 fl oz/scant ⅓ cup plain
  yogurt
100 ml/3½ fl oz/scant ½ cup
  milk
115 g/4 oz/½ cup soft brown
  sugar
6 tbsp sunflower oil
2 apples, peeled, cored and finely
  diced

For the cinnamon butter
115 g/4 oz butter, at room
  temperature
60 g/2 oz/⅓ cup icing sugar,
  sifted
1 tsp ground cinnamon

Preheat the oven to 200°C/400°F/Gas 6. Grease or line a 12-hole muffin pan.

Combine the flour, bicarbonate of soda and cinnamon and sift into a large bowl.

In a separate bowl, combine the eggs, yogurt, milk, brown sugar and oil, then stir in the apples. Pour the mixture into the dry ingredients and stir together until just combined, then spoon big dollops of the mixture into the prepared muffin pan.

Bake for about 20 minutes until risen and golden. Leave to cool in the pan for a couple of minutes, then transfer to a wire rack to cool.

Meanwhile, beat together the butter, icing sugar and cinnamon. Serve the muffins warm, with the cinnamon butter for spreading.

Nutty banana and choc chip chomps

Throwing a handful of white chocolate chips into this old favourite adds a spot of wicked indulgence just where you need it. Eat them while they're still warm to really enjoy the oozing stickiness of the melted chocolate inside. Yum!

✹ Makes 12

300 g/10 oz/2 cups plain flour
1 tbsp baking powder
85 g/3 oz/scant ½ cup soft brown
    sugar
150 ml/5 fl oz/scant ⅔ cup milk
1 egg, beaten
100 ml/3½ fl oz/scant ½ cup
    sunflower oil
2 ripe bananas, roughly mashed
85 g/3 oz/⅔ cup walnut pieces
100 g/3½ oz white chocolate
    chips

Preheat the oven to 200°C/400°F/Gas 6. Grease or line a 12-hole muffin pan.

Combine the flour and baking powder and sift into a large bowl.

In a separate bowl, combine the sugar, milk, egg, oil and bananas, then stir in the nuts and chocolate chips and tip into the dry ingredients. Stir together until just combined, then spoon big dollops of the mixture into the prepared muffin pan.

Bake for about 20 minutes until risen and golden. Leave to cool in the pan for a few minutes, then transfer to a wire rack to cool.

Blueberry bliss

Is it those dark purply berries oozing juice, or the tender vanilla crumb that makes this classic such a favourite? Eat them still warm from the oven to enjoy them at their very best. This simple recipe is made without eggs so that anyone with an egg allergy doesn't have to miss out!

✱ Makes 12

300 g/10 oz/2 cups self-raising flour
1 tsp baking powder
85 g/3 oz/scant ½ cup caster sugar
150 g/5 oz/1 cup blueberries, plus a few extra for decoration
225 ml/8 fl oz/scant 1 cup buttermilk (or a mixture of half milk, half yogurt)
1 tsp vanilla essence
85 g/3 oz butter, melted

✱ You will find these pictured on p.15.

Preheat the oven to 200°C/400°F/Gas 6. Grease or line a 12-hole muffin pan.

Combine the flour, baking powder and sugar and sift into a large bowl, then add the blueberries.

In a separate bowl or jug, combine the buttermilk, vanilla and butter, then pour into the dry ingredients. Stir together gently until just combined, then spoon big dollops of the mixture into the prepared muffin pan. Press a few extra blueberries into the tops of the muffins so there's a generous number on the top.

Bake for about 20 minutes until risen and golden. Leave to cool in the pan for a few minutes, then transfer to a wire rack to cool.

Spiced maple and pecan munchies

Another irresistible combination that you can throw together in minutes and be munching on in less than half an hour. (And although they're pretty good cold ... you probably won't be able to leave them on the wire rack long enough to find out!)

✳ Makes 12

300 g/10 oz/2 cups self-raising flour
1 tsp baking powder
125 g/4½ oz/generous ½ cup caster sugar
½ tsp mixed spice
75 g/2¾ oz pecan nuts, roughly chopped, plus extra for sprinkling
2 eggs, beaten
75 ml/3 fl oz/scant ⅓ cup milk
100 ml/3½ fl oz/scant ½ cup plain yogurt
4 tbsp maple syrup, plus extra for brushing
85 g/3 oz butter, melted

Preheat the oven to 190°C/375°F/Gas 5. Grease or line a 12-hole muffin pan.

Combine the flour, baking powder, sugar and mixed spice and sift into a large bowl, then add the nuts.

In a separate bowl or jug, combine the eggs, milk, yogurt and syrup, then stir in the butter. Pour into the dry ingredients and stir together until just mixed. Spoon big dollops of the mixture into the prepared muffin pan and sprinkle over a few more chopped pecan nuts.

Bake for about 20 minutes until risen and golden. Leave to cool in the pan for a few minutes, then transfer to a wire rack. While still warm, brush with more maple syrup.

Lemon and almond crumbles

Lemony, almondy, moist, moreish ... what's not to like? These are another of those easy-peasy muffins that somehow elicit an air of sophistication and make you feel rather ladylike – until you find yourself trying to resist the urge to eat more than one!

✳ Makes 12

225 g/8 oz/1½ cups self-raising flour
1 tsp baking powder
150 g/5 oz/⅔ cup caster sugar
115 g/4 oz/1 cup ground almonds
1 egg, beaten
225 ml/8 fl oz/scant 1 cup milk
85 g/3 oz butter, melted
grated zest of 2 lemons
40 g/1½ oz/½ cup flaked almonds, for sprinkling
icing sugar, for dusting

Preheat the oven to 200°C/400°F/Gas 6. Grease or line a 12-hole muffin pan.

Combine the flour, baking powder and caster sugar and sift into a large bowl. Sprinkle the ground almonds into the bowl.

In a separate bowl or jug, combine the egg, milk, butter and lemon zest, then pour into the dry ingredients. Stir together until just combined, then spoon big dollops of the mixture into the prepared muffin pan. Sprinkle the tops with flaked almonds.

Bake for about 20 minutes until risen and golden. Leave to cool in the pan for a few minutes, then transfer to a wire rack to cool. Serve dusted with icing sugar.

Date and ginger honeys

Topped off with lashings of sticky honey and creamy crème fraîche, these gluten-free muffins are messy to eat, but all the better for it! Eat them while they're still warm, using a teaspoon to scoop the muffin and toppings out of the paper case. Alternatively, just serve with a lot of napkins!

✳ Makes 12

200 g/7 oz/1⅓ cup potato flour
100 g/3½ oz/⅔ cup rice flour
1 tbsp baking powder
1 tsp ground ginger
2 eggs, beaten
100 ml/3½ fl oz/scant ½ cup
   plain yogurt
75 ml/3 fl oz/scant ⅓ cup milk
5 tbsp vegetable oil
115 g/4 oz/½ cup brown sugar
100 g/3½ oz pitted dates, roughly
   chopped
3 pieces stem ginger in syrup,
   roughly chopped
clear honey, for drizzling
crème fraîche, for dolloping

Preheat the oven to 200°C/400°F/Gas 6. Line a 12-hole muffin pan.

Combine the flours, baking powder and ginger and sift into a large bowl.

In a separate bowl, lightly beat together the eggs, yogurt, milk, oil and sugar, then stir in the dates and about two-thirds of the stem ginger. Pour into the dry ingredients and stir together until just combined. Spoon big dollops of the mixture into the prepared muffin pan and sprinkle the remaining pieces of ginger over the top.

Bake for about 20 minutes until risen and golden. Leave to cool in the pan for a few minutes, then transfer to a wire rack to cool.

Serve slightly warm, drizzled with honey and topped with a generous dollop of crème fraîche.

Tangy rhubarb and custard

For that old-fashioned pud feel, serve these moist, tender muffins warm, topped with a big spoonful of thick, fresh custard. They'll be messy to eat, but worth getting sticky fingers for!

✳ Makes 12

300 g/10 oz/2 cups self-raising
   flour
1 tsp baking powder
1 tsp ground ginger
50 g/1¾ oz/4 tbsp mascarpone
125 ml/4 fl oz/½ cup milk
2 eggs, beaten
150 g/5 oz/⅔ cup soft brown
   sugar
115 g/4 oz butter, melted
175 g/6 oz rhubarb, chopped
ready-made custard, to serve
   (optional)

Preheat the oven to 200°C/400°F/Gas 6. Grease or line a 12-hole muffin pan.

Combine the flour, baking powder and ginger and sift into a large bowl.

In a separate bowl, beat the mascarpone until soft, then gradually beat in 1–2 tbsp milk until smooth and creamy, then beat in the rest with the eggs. Stir in the sugar and butter, then add the rhubarb and pour into the dry ingredients. Stir together until just combined, then spoon dollops of the mixture into the prepared muffin pan.

Bake for about 20 minutes until risen and golden. Leave to cool in the pan for a few minutes, then transfer to a wire rack to cool.

Serve on their own, or topped with a big dollop of fresh custard.

Muesli morning muffins

When you're after a dairy-free brekkie, these wholesome muffins are the way to go. Packed with oats, dried fruit and seeds, they're substantial little devils – and not too sweet – so you could almost feel like you're being healthy! (And, of course, if you're happy drinking milk, you can use regular milk in place of the soya milk.)

✳ Makes 12

250 g/9 oz/1⅔ cups self-raising flour
1 tsp baking powder
1 tsp ground ginger
100 g/3½ oz/½ cup muesli
2 tbsp pumpkin seeds
50 g/1¾ oz ready-to-eat dried apricots, chopped
2 eggs, beaten
200 ml/7 fl oz/generous ¾ cup soya milk
5 tbsp sunflower oil
50 g/1¾ oz/¼ cup soft brown sugar
5 tbsp clear honey

Preheat the oven to 200°C/400°F/Gas 6. Grease or line a 12-hole muffin pan.

Combine the flour, baking powder and ginger and sift into a large bowl.

In a separate bowl, combine the muesli and pumpkin seeds, then set aside about one-quarter of the mixture. Add the remaining muesli mixture and apricots to the flour.

In a separate bowl or jug, combine the eggs, milk, oil, sugar and honey, stirring until the honey is well mixed. Pour into the dry ingredients and stir together until just combined. Spoon big dollops of the mixture into the prepared muffin pan and sprinkle the remaining muesli mixture over the top.

Bake for about 20 minutes until risen and golden. Leave to cool in the pan for a couple of minutes, then transfer to a wire rack to cool.

Spotty dotty orange and poppy seed

Fresh, zesty and not too sweet, these little rascals are just right for a lazy weekend breakfast. Serve them warm with a mug of freshly brewed coffee, and if you're feeling extra-naughty, try them with a spoonful of crème fraîche and a dollop of orange curd on top.

✸ Makes 12

300 g/10 oz/2 cups plain flour
1 tbsp baking powder
115 g/4 oz/½ cup caster sugar
2 tbsp poppy seeds
1 egg, beaten
100 ml/3½ fl oz/generous ⅓ cup
   plain yogurt
3 tbsp milk
50 g/1¾ oz butter, melted
grated zest and juice of 2 oranges

✸ You will find these pictured on
   the front cover.

Preheat the oven to 200°C/400°F/Gas 6. Grease or line a 12-hole muffin pan.

Combine the flour, baking powder, sugar and poppy seeds and sift into a large bowl.

In a separate bowl or jug, lightly beat together the egg, yogurt and milk to combine, then stir in the butter and orange juice and zest. Pour into the dry ingredients and stir together until just combined, then spoon big dollops of the mixture into the prepared muffin pan.

Bake for about 20 minutes until risen and golden. Leave to cool in the pan for a few minutes, then transfer to a wire rack to cool.

Kiddie-friendly

2

Kids love muffins. I don't know if it's something about the individual size of muffins, the pretty paper wrapper, or the big puffy top that makes them so appealing to young people (and old, now I come to think of it!), or maybe it's the fact that they're so easy to make that even really young kids can help out with the stirring and dolloping. Whatever the secret of their appeal, this chapter is dedicated to muffins that youngsters just won't be able to resist.

There's a mixture of recipes – from easy-peasy ones that they can make themselves with just a bit of adult supervision, to ridiculously fun and frivolous ones covered in frosting and coloured candy. There are some healthier options, too, using a bit less fat and a bit less sugar, so that you can give your kids a well-deserved treat without feeling fraught with the worry that you're filling their little bodies with toxic ingredients that will leave their heads spinning and their behaviour a little less cooperative than might be desired.

Jammy donuts

Easy-peasy to make, but kids will love you for them! And they'll love you even more if you let them help you. Little kids can help with dolloping muffin mixture and jam, while older kids can do it all themselves with just a bit of grown-up supervision. These are best served slightly warm, but do let them cool a bit first as the jam inside can be hot.

✳ Makes 12

300 g/10 oz/2 cups self-raising
    flour
1 tsp baking powder
150 g/5 oz/⅔ cup caster sugar,
    plus extra for dredging
250 ml/9 fl oz/1 cup buttermilk
1 egg, beaten
50 g/1¾ oz butter, melted
1 tsp vanilla essence
4 tbsp raspberry jam

Preheat the oven to 200°C/400°F/Gas 6. Grease or line a 12-hole muffin pan.

Combine the flour, baking powder and sugar and sift into a large bowl.

In a separate bowl or jug, combine the buttermilk, egg, butter and vanilla, then pour into the dry ingredients. Spoon small dollops of the mixture into the prepared muffin pan. Using the back of a teaspoon, make an indent in the mixture and drop in a teaspoonful of jam, then top with more mixture.

Bake for about 20 minutes until risen and golden. Leave to cool in the pan for a few minutes, then transfer to a wire rack to cool. While still warm, sprinkle caster sugar over each muffin so they look like a little batch of freshly fried donuts.

Peanut butter and choc chip cheekies

Kids just love these big fat muffins studded with chocolate chips and little nuggets of peanut. Throw a batch in the oven after school and they can enjoy them warm with a big glass of milk. If you want to go for a dairy-free version, use plain chocolate chips and substitute soya milk for regular milk.

✳ Makes 12

300 g/10 oz/2 cups self-raising flour
1 tsp baking powder
100 g/3½ oz milk chocolate chips
200 g/7 oz/generous ⅔ cup crunchy peanut butter
115 g/4 oz/½ cup soft brown sugar
2 eggs, beaten
200 ml/7 fl oz/generous ¾ cup milk

Preheat the oven to 200°C/400°F/Gas 6. Grease or line a 12-hole muffin pan.

Combine the flour and baking powder and sift into a large bowl, then add about three-quarters of the chocolate chips.

In a separate bowl, beat together the peanut butter and sugar, then gradually beat in the eggs and milk to make a smooth mixture. Pour into the dry ingredients and stir together until just combined, then spoon large dollops into the prepared muffin pan. Sprinkle with the remaining chocolate chips, pressing them gently into the mixture.

Bake for about 18 minutes until risen and golden. Leave to cool in the pan for a few minutes, then transfer to a wire rack to cool.

Mini fruit marvels

These cute little fruity numbers are just irresistible for mini hands and make a great tea party standard. Mix up the icing and let the kids decorate them themselves, then lay the table (or picnic rug if you're going down the teddy bear's picnic route) and have an afternoon of fun. (And if your kids don't like mixed peel, just leave it out!)

✱ Makes 24

150 g/5 oz/1 cup self-raising
    flour
½ tsp baking powder
4 tbsp caster sugar
75 ml/2½ fl oz/scant ⅓ cup milk
3 tbsp plain yogurt
1 egg, beaten
40 g/1½ oz butter, melted
grated zest of 1 orange
60 g/2 oz/6 tbsp raisins,
    plus extra to decorate
2 tbsp mixed candied peel,
    plus extra to decorate
60 g/2 oz/⅓ cup icing sugar,
    sifted
1½–2 tsp orange juice

Preheat the oven to 190°C/375°F/Gas 5. Line two 12-hole mini muffin pans with mini muffin papers.

Combine the flour, baking powder and caster sugar and sift into a large bowl.

In a separate bowl, lightly beat together the milk, yogurt and egg to combine, then stir in the butter, orange zest and dried fruit and peel. Pour into the dry ingredients and stir until just combined, then spoon dollops of the mixture into the prepared muffin pans.

Bake for about 15 minutes until risen and golden. Leave to cool in the pans for a few minutes, then transfer to a wire rack to cool.

To decorate, mix the icing sugar and orange juice until smooth, then spoon on to the cooled muffins. Decorate each one with a raisin or a few pieces of mixed peel.

Beetroot bonanza

Don't be put off if you don't like beetroot, these perfectly pink muffins are not a million miles away from a carrot-cakey muffin – sweet, tender, moreish and, even better, bright pink! Serve them with a simple swirl of frosting or, for something a bit more special, look out for pink sugar sprinkles to scatter over the top.

✳ Makes 12

300 g/10 oz/2 cups plain flour
1 tbsp baking powder
150 g/5 oz/⅔ cup caster sugar
1 tsp ground cinnamon
½ tsp ground ginger
200 ml/7 fl oz/generous ¾ cup milk
2 large eggs, beaten
100 ml/3½ fl oz/scant ½ cup vegetable oil
largish beetroot, grated (about 100 g/3½ oz)

For the frosting
150 g/5 oz cream cheese
4½ tbsp icing sugar
1 tsp lemon juice
pink food colouring

Preheat the oven to 200°C/400°F/Gas 6. Grease or line a 12-hole muffin pan.

Combine the flour, baking powder, caster sugar, cinnamon and ginger and sift into a large bowl.

In a separate bowl, combine the milk, eggs and oil, then stir in the beetroot so that the mixture turns bright pink. Pour into the dry ingredients and stir together until just combined, then spoon large dollops of the mixture into the prepared muffin pan.

Bake for about 20 minutes until risen and firm to the touch. Leave to cool in the pan for a few minutes, then transfer to a wire rack to cool.

To serve, beat together the cream cheese, icing sugar and lemon juice until smooth and creamy. Add a few drops of pink food colouring to make a vibrant pink frosting, then swirl on top of the muffins.

Coloured candies

These muffins are kiddie-tastic and will appeal to really little ones as much as older kids – particularly the way the candies turn the muffins rainbow-coloured once they've been baked. Little-uns can help out with spooning on the frosting and sticking on sweeties, while older kids can pretty much do it all themselves.

✳ Makes 12

300 g/10 oz/2 cups self-raising flour
1 tsp baking powder
115 g/4 oz/½ cup caster sugar
60 g/2 oz Smarties or M&Ms
200 ml/7 fl oz/generous ¾ cup buttermilk
1 egg, beaten
1 tsp vanilla essence
85 g/3 oz butter, melted

To decorate
75 ml/2½ fl oz/scant ⅓ cup soured cream
100 g/3½ oz/1 cup icing sugar, sifted
60 g/2 oz Smarties or M&Ms

Preheat the oven to 190°C/375°F/Gas 5. Grease or line a 12-hole muffin pan.

Combine the flour, baking powder and caster sugar and sift into a large bowl, then add the Smarties or M&Ms.

In a separate bowl or jug, lightly beat the buttermilk, egg and vanilla to combine, then stir in the butter. Pour into the dry ingredients and stir together until just combined, then spoon big dollops of the mixture into the prepared muffin pan.

Bake for about 20 minutes until risen and golden. Leave to cool in the pan for a few minutes, then transfer to a wire rack to cool.

To decorate, beat the soured cream and icing sugar together until creamy, then spoon over the muffins. Decorate with more Smarties or M&Ms on top.

Vanilla fudgies

Eat these gorgeous muffins while they're still warm to really enjoy the squidgy, soft fudge chunks at their best, but have a little patience, too, and let them cool slightly first so the fudge isn't too hot. You can use any type of fudge you like – vanilla fudge, chocolate fudge, raisin fudge, or whatever else you can lay your hands on. Just chop it up, chuck it in and wait for your muffins to bake.

✳ Makes 12

300 g/10 oz/2 cups self-raising flour
1 tsp baking powder
115 g/4 oz/½ cup caster sugar
100 g/3½ oz fudge, cut into pieces
125 ml/4 fl oz/½ cup milk
100 ml/3½ fl oz/scant ½ cup half-fat crème fraîche
1 egg, beaten
1 tsp vanilla essence
60 g/2 oz butter, melted

Preheat the oven to 200°C/400°F/Gas 6. Grease or line a 12-hole muffin pan.

Combine the flour, baking powder and sugar and sift into a large bowl, then scatter the fudge on top.

In a separate bowl or jug, lightly beat the milk, crème fraîche, egg and vanilla until smooth, then stir in the butter. Pour into the dry ingredients and mix together until just combined, then spoon big dollops of the mixture into the prepared muffin pan.

Bake for about 20 minutes until risen and golden. Leave to cool in the pan for a few minutes, then transfer to a wire rack to cool.

Honey-nut muffins

Simple and sticky, these moreish golden muffins rely on honey and unrefined brown sugar for their sweetness. For a lunchbox treat, brush them with a little honey while warm, but leave out the extra drizzling so they're not too sticky when it gets to lunchtime. If your kids like things a little bit spicy, try throwing in a touch of ground cinnamon as well.

✳ Makes 12

300 g/10 oz/2 cups self-raising flour
1 tsp baking powder
1 tsp ground cinnamon (optional)
85 g/3 oz/⅔ cup roughly chopped nuts, such as walnuts, pistachio nuts and hazelnuts, plus extra for sprinkling
225 ml/8 fl oz/scant 1 cup milk
1 egg, beaten
4 tbsp clear honey, plus extra for drizzling
100 g/3½ oz/scant ½ cup soft brown sugar
85 g/3 oz butter, melted

Preheat the oven to 200°C/400°F/Gas 6. Grease or line a 12-hole muffin pan.

Combine the flour and baking powder and add the cinnamon, if you like, and sift into a large bowl, then add the nuts.

In a separate bowl or jug, combine the milk, egg and honey and stir until the honey has dissolved. Stir in the sugar and butter, then pour into the dry ingredients and stir until just combined. Spoon large dollops of the mixture into the prepared muffin pan and sprinkle more chopped nuts on top.

Bake for about 20 minutes until risen and golden. Leave to cool in the pan for a few minutes, then transfer to a wire rack to cool.

Serve while still warm, drizzled with honey.

Peppermint stick muffins

Let the kids help you make these magnificently minty muffins. They'll love bashing the mints to break them up, and save you a lot of energy! Look out for stripy sticks of rock or candy cane and tint the frosting in a contrasting colour to really make them stand out.

❋ Makes 12

300 g/10 oz/2 cups self-raising flour
1 tsp baking powder
85 g/3 oz/⅓ cup caster sugar
2 packets of extra strong mints (40 g/1½ oz each)
2 eggs, beaten
225 ml/8 fl oz/scant 1 cup milk
85 g/3 oz butter, melted

To decorate
3 sticks of peppermint candy cane or rock (about 85 g/3 oz)
200 g/7 oz/1¾ cups icing sugar, sifted
2 tbsp lemon juice
food colouring (optional)

Preheat the oven to 200°C/400°F/Gas 6. Grease or line a 12-hole muffin pan.

Combine the flour, baking powder and caster sugar, then sift into a bowl. Put the mints in a mortar and pound with a pestle to break them up into small pieces. Scatter them over the flour.

In a separate bowl or jug, lightly beat together the eggs and milk to combine, then stir in the butter. Pour into the dry ingredients and stir together until just combined, then spoon dollops of the mixture into the prepared muffin pan.

Bake for about 20 minutes until risen and golden. Leave to cool in the pan for a few minutes, then transfer to a wire rack to cool.

To decorate, put the candy cane or rock in a plastic bag and tap with a rolling pin to break into pieces. Set aside. Stir together the sugar and lemon juice until smooth, then add a few drops of food colouring to tint the icing, if you like. Spoon on top of the muffins and sprinkle pieces of candy cane or rock on top.

Birthday mini muffins

Who needs a birthday cake when there are mini muffins to gobble instead? With twenty-four muffins in each batch, they're just perfect for a party – or for a very greedy birthday boy or girl!

✳ Makes 24

300 g/10 oz/2 cups self-raising flour
1 tsp baking powder
2 tbsp cocoa powder, plus extra for dusting
150 g/5 oz/⅔ cup caster sugar
100 g/3½ oz dark chocolate, chopped
1 egg, beaten
250 ml/9 fl oz/1 cup plain yogurt
2 tbsp milk
85 g/3 oz butter, melted
24 birthday candles, to decorate

Preheat the oven to 190°C/375°F/Gas 5. Grease or line a 24-hole mini muffin pan.

Combine the flour, baking powder, cocoa and caster sugar and sift into a large bowl, then add the chocolate.

In a separate bowl or jug, combine the egg, yogurt, milk and butter, then pour into the dry ingredients. Stir together until just combined, then spoon large dollops of the mixture into the prepared muffin pan, making sure there are plenty of chocolate chunks peeping through the tops of the muffins.

Bake for about 15 minutes until risen and firm to the touch. Leave to cool in the pan for a few minutes, then transfer to a wire rack to cool completely.

To serve, dust with cocoa and stick a candle in the centre of each muffin. Light and enjoy!

Figgy oatmeal muffins

Sweet, sticky and great for kids on a dairy-free diet. Although having said that, kids who do eat milk and butter will love these too, and mums and dads, and grandparents...

✳ Makes 12

50 g/1¾ oz/½ cup rolled oats
150 g/5 oz ready-to-eat dried figs, chopped
125 ml/4 fl oz/½ cup boiling water
250 g/9 oz/1⅔ cups self-raising flour
1 tsp baking powder
115 g/4 oz/½ cup caster sugar
2 eggs, beaten
150 ml/5 fl oz/scant ⅔ cup soya milk
6 tbsp sunflower oil

For the topping
75 g/2¾ oz ready-to-eat dried figs, chopped
3 tbsp clear honey
2 tsp boiling water

Preheat the oven to 200°C/400°F/Gas 6. Line a 12-hole muffin pan.

Put the oats and figs in a bowl and pour over the boiling water. Leave to soak for 10 minutes.

Combine the flour, baking powder and sugar and sift into a large bowl.

Add the eggs, milk and oil to the soaked oats and lightly beat together until combined, then pour into the dry ingredients. Stir together until just mixed, then spoon big dollops of the mixture into the prepared muffin pan.

Bake for about 20 minutes until risen and golden. Leave to cool in the pan for a few minutes, then transfer to a wire rack to cool.

While the muffins are still warm, make the topping. Put the figs, honey and water in a pan and simmer for about 1 minute. Spoon over the muffins and leave to cool.

Rocky roadsters

Although the rocky road combination of nuts, marshmallows and chocolate usually goes into ice cream, there's no reason why you shouldn't throw the trio into a muffin instead. If you do, you'll find yourself with an irresistible batch of the squishiest, melty-est, chunkiest muffins you've ever seen.

✳ Makes 12

300 g/10 oz/2 cups self-raising flour
1 tsp baking powder
3 tbsp cocoa powder
75 g/2¾ oz milk chocolate, chopped
60 g/2 oz/½ cup walnut pieces
60 g/2 oz mini marshmallows (or large marshmallows snipped into pieces)
150 g/5 oz/⅔ cup soft brown sugar
200 ml/7 fl oz/generous ¾ cup milk
2 eggs, beaten
75 g/2¾ oz butter, melted

Preheat the oven to 200°C/400°F/Gas 6. Grease or line a 12-hole muffin pan.

Combine the flour, baking powder and cocoa and sift into a large bowl. Reserve about one-third of the chocolate chunks and nuts, then add the rest, along with the marshmallows, to the flour.

In a separate bowl or jug, combine the sugar, milk, eggs and butter, then pour into the dry ingredients. Stir together until just combined, then spoon big dollops of the mixture into the prepared muffin pan. Gently press the reserved chocolate and nuts at random into the muffins.

Bake for about 20 minutes until risen and firm to the touch. Leave to cool in the pan for a few minutes, then transfer to a wire rack to cool.

Tropical temptations

Go exotic with these fabulously fruity muffins oozing with melting mango and tangy pineapple. Turn the heating right up, shut your eyes and imagine you're on a tropical island ... eating a muffin!

✳ **Makes 12**

300 g/10 oz/2 cups self-raising flour
1 tsp baking powder
150 g/5 oz/⅔ cup caster sugar
1 egg, beaten
100 ml/3½ fl oz/scant ½ cup crème fraîche
125 ml/4 fl oz/½ cup milk
grated zest of 1 lime
85 g/3 oz butter, melted
115 g/4 oz mango flesh, diced
75 g/2¾ oz pineapple, diced

Preheat the oven to 200°C/400°F/Gas 6. Grease or line a 12-hole muffin pan. Combine the flour, baking powder and sugar and sift into a large bowl.

In a separate bowl, briefly beat the egg, crème fraîche, milk and lime zest until smooth, then stir in the butter and about three-quarters of the mango and pineapple. Add to the dry ingredients and stir together until just combined. Spoon large dollops of the mixture into the prepared muffin pan, then top each muffin with the remaining mango and pineapple.

Bake for about 20 minutes until risen and golden. Leave to cool in the pan for a few minutes, then transfer to a wire rack to cool.

Adults only

3

All right, I'll be honest, it's hard to make a really mature muffin. In fact, I think there's probably something inherently rather immature about your average muffin. You'll never find a muffin nestling on the shelf of a sophisticated Parisian pâtisserie, but that doesn't mean you can't make muffins that really should be enjoyed only by an adult audience. I'm talking decadence here, and things far too good to be wasted on young palates that aren't quite mature enough to appreciate them properly – chocolate, whipped cream, oozingly velvety *dulce de leche*, almonds, raspberries, rum, and all those other things that are just too, too good!

Some of these muffins are so seductively indulgent and moreish, so tantalisingly naughty, so lusciously lush that they'll make even the most mature of grown-ups flutter and blush in their presence. These muffins are about full-on indulgence. The kind of indulgence where you need to shut the door, make yourself very comfortable and dedicate just a bit of time to you and your muffin. Don't hold back on these ones, just relax and let the muffins do their work.

Espresso express

Make these in the morning when you need a bit of jet-fuel to get you going. After munching your way through the coffee-flavoured crumb specked with whole chocolate-covered coffee beans and all topped off with a lusciously creamy, sugary coffee buttercream, nothing's going to stop you!

✳ Makes 12

300 g/10 oz/2 cups plain flour
1 tbsp baking powder
150 g/5 oz/⅔ cup caster sugar
40 g/1½ oz/¼ cup chocolate-
    covered coffee beans
1 egg, beaten
175 ml/6 fl oz/¾ cup milk
2 tbsp Greek yogurt
2 tbsp instant coffee, dissolved in
    2 tbsp boiling water
85 g/3 oz butter, melted

For the topping
100 g/3½ oz butter, at room
    temperature
200 g/7 oz/1¾ cups icing sugar,
    sifted
2 tsp instant coffee, dissolved in
    1 tbsp boiling water
chocolate-covered coffee beans,
    to decorate

Preheat the oven to 200°C/400°F/Gas 6. Grease or line a 12-hole muffin pan.

Combine the flour, baking powder and caster sugar and sift into a large bowl, then scatter the coffee beans on top.

In a separate bowl or jug, lightly beat together the egg, milk, yogurt and coffee, then stir in the melted butter. Pour into the dry ingredients and stir together until just combined, then spoon big dollops of the mixture into the prepared muffin pan.

Bake for about 20 minutes until risen and firm to the touch. Leave to cool in the pan for a few minutes, then transfer to a wire rack to cool completely.

To decorate, beat together the butter, icing sugar and coffee until smooth and creamy. Swirl on top of the muffins and decorate with more chocolate-covered coffee beans.

Banoffee toffees

Just like the pie ... but a bit more muffiny! There's something just irresistible about the decadent combination of whipped cream, bananas and gooey, sticky, velvety toffee sauce, which makes these magical muffins the only ones to choose when you need a little bit of comfort muffin in your life.

✳ Makes 12

300 g/10 oz/2 cups plain flour
1 tbsp baking powder
1 egg, beaten
200 ml/7 fl oz/generous ¾ cup milk
150 g/5 oz/⅔ cup soft brown sugar
85 g/3 oz butter, melted
2 bananas, peeled and diced

To decorate
150 ml/5 fl oz/⅔ cup double cream
1–2 bananas, sliced
4 tbsp *dulce de leche*

Preheat the oven to 200°C/400°F/Gas 6. Grease or line a 12-hole muffin pan.

Combine the flour and baking powder and sift into a large bowl.

In a separate bowl or jug, combine the egg and milk, then stir in the sugar and melted butter. Add the banana, give it all a quick stir, then tip into the dry ingredients and stir together until just mixed. Spoon big dollops of the mixture into the prepared muffin pan.

Bake for about 20 minutes until risen and golden. Leave to cool in the pan for a few minutes, then transfer to a wire rack to cool completely.

To decorate, whip the cream until it stands in soft peaks, then spoon dollops on top of each muffin. Top with a couple of slices of banana, drizzle with *dulce de leche* and serve.

Triple choc-chunkies

This is the muffin for all you chocaholics out there. A chocolatey crumb, then big chunks of white and dark chocolate inside – and if you serve them while they're still warm, that chocolate is oh-so-gooey, and oh-so-good!

✳ Makes 12

300 g/10 oz/2 cups plain flour
1 tbsp baking powder
3 tbsp cocoa powder
150 g/5 oz/⅔ cup caster sugar
75 g/2¾ oz dark chocolate, chopped
75 g/2¾ oz white chocolate, chopped
2 eggs
125 ml/4 fl oz/½ cup soured cream
100 ml/3½ fl oz/scant ½ cup milk
85 g/3 oz butter, melted

✳ You will find these pictured on p.59.

Preheat the oven to 200°C/400°F/Gas 6. Grease or line a 12-hole muffin pan.

Combine the flour, baking powder, cocoa and sugar and sift into a large bowl. Reserve about 25 g/1 oz of the dark chocolate chunks and add the rest of the dark and white chocolate to the sifted ingredients.

In a separate bowl or jug, lightly beat together the eggs, cream and milk until smooth, then stir in the butter and pour into the dry ingredients. Stir together until just combined, then spoon large dollops of the mixture into the prepared muffin pan. Top the muffins with the reserved chunks of chocolate, pressing them gently into the mixture.

Bake for about 20 minutes until risen and firm to the touch. Leave to cool in the pan for a few minutes, then transfer to a wire rack to cool.

White chocolate, cherry and macadamia

These cheeky little numbers are just the right side of decadent indulgence. Not so naughty that you need to feel guilty, but just sweet and sticky enough to give you the feel-good hit you deserve. Slightly sharp cherries, sweet, melted white chocolate and perfectly round, nutty macadamias ... what's not to like?

✳ Makes 12

300 g/10 oz/2 cups plain flour
1 tbsp baking powder
150 g/5 oz/⅔ cup caster sugar
75 g/2¾ oz white chocolate, chopped
60 g/2 oz/½ cup dried cherries
60 g/2 oz/½ cup macadamia nuts
1 egg, beaten
100 ml/3½ fl oz/scant ½ cup soured cream
125 ml/4 fl oz/½ cup milk
85 g/3 oz butter, melted

Preheat the oven to 190°C/375°F/Gas 5. Grease or line a 12-hole muffin pan.

Combine the flour, baking powder and sugar and sift into a large bowl. Reserve about one-quarter each of the chocolate, cherries and nuts and add the rest to the flour.

In a separate bowl or jug, lightly beat the egg, soured cream and milk to combine, then stir in the butter. Pour into the dry ingredients and stir together until just combined. Spoon large dollops of the mixture into the prepared muffin pan and press the reserved chocolate, cherries and nuts into the top of each.

Bake for about 20 minutes until risen and golden. Leave to cool in the pan for a few minutes, then transfer to a wire rack to cool.

Chocolate hazelnut melts

There's something a little bit childish about these muffins filled with Nutella, which are gorgeously gooey and sticky when you bite into them – but they're too good for kids! Bake yourself a batch, put on the coffee and sit back and relax in utter decadence!

✹ Makes 12

100 g/3½ oz/scant 1 cup toasted hazelnuts, plus extra to decorate
200 g/7 oz/1⅓ cups plain flour
1 tbsp baking powder
3 tbsp cocoa powder
150 g/5 oz/⅔ cup caster sugar
1 egg, beaten
200 ml/7 fl oz/generous ¾ cup buttermilk
2 tbsp milk
85 g/3 oz butter, melted
4 tbsp Nutella or other chocolate and hazelnut spread

Preheat the oven to 190°C/375°F/Gas 5. Grease or line a 12-hole muffin pan. Put the nuts in a food processor and process until finely ground.

Combine the ground nuts with the flour, baking powder, cocoa and sugar and sift into a large bowl. (Don't worry if all the nuts don't go through, just sprinkle them over the top.)

In a separate bowl or jug, combine the egg, buttermilk and milk, then stir in the butter. Pour into the dry ingredients and stir together until just combined, then spoon small dollops of the mixture into the prepared muffin pan. Using the back of a teaspoon, make a slight indent in the mixture and spoon 1 teaspoon Nutella into the centre of each muffin. Top with the remaining mixture and press a few whole hazelnuts into the top of each one.

Bake for about 20 minutes until risen and firm to the touch. Leave to cool in the pan for a few minutes, then transfer to a wire rack to cool.

Luscious lemon and raspberry

Just because you're avoiding gluten, doesn't mean you need to miss out on indulging yourself in a muffin now and again. Tender, sweet, lemony, fruity and creamy, you'll never feel deprived once you've baked a batch of these beauties! The raspberries sink to the bottom to create a dense, moist, fruity layer, topped off with a light, almondy crumb. For something simpler, just leave out the topping and serve plain.

✱ Makes 12

100 g/3½ oz/1 cup ground
   almonds
100 g/3½ oz/⅔ cup potato flour
50 g/1¾ oz/⅓ cup rice flour
150 g/5 oz/⅔ cup caster sugar
1 tbsp gluten-free baking powder
150 g/5 oz/1 cup raspberries
2 eggs, beaten
175 ml/6 fl oz/¾ cup milk
85 g/3 oz butter, melted
grated zest of 1 lemon

For the topping
150 g/5 oz mascarpone
6 tbsp gluten-free lemon curd
fresh raspberries, to decorate

Preheat the oven to 200°C/400°F/Gas 6. Line a 12-hole muffin pan with paper cases.

Combine the ground almonds, potato and rice flours, the sugar and baking powder and sift into a large bowl. (Don't worry if there are still some large bits of ground almond left in the sieve, just sprinkle them over the top.) Add the raspberries.

In a separate bowl or jug, combine the eggs, milk, butter and lemon zest, then pour into the dry ingredients and gently stir together – being careful not to break up the raspberries – until the ingredients are just mixed. Spoon big dollops of the mixture into the prepared muffin pan.

Bake for about 18 minutes until risen and golden. Leave to cool in the pan for a few minutes, then transfer to a wire rack to cool completely.

To decorate, beat together the mascarpone and lemon curd until creamy, then swirl on top of the cakes and decorate with fresh raspberries.

Rum-raisin rumba

Light, crumbly and golden with a distinctive kick of rum, these are definitely not a breakfast muffin! Serve them plain or top with a spoonful of mascarpone or a dusting of icing sugar.

✳ Makes 12

115 g/4 oz/¾ cup raisins
3 tbsp dark rum
300 g/10 oz/2 cups self-raising flour
1 tsp baking powder
150 g/5 oz/⅔ cup caster sugar
1 egg, beaten
75 ml/3 fl oz/scant ⅓ cup milk
100 ml/3½ fl oz/scant ½ cup soured cream
85 g/3 oz butter, melted

Put the raisins and rum in a bowl and leave to soak for 1 hour.

Preheat the oven to 200°C/400°F/Gas 6. Grease or line a 12-hole muffin pan.

Combine the flour, baking powder and sugar and sift into a large bowl.

In a separate bowl or jug, lightly beat together the egg, milk and soured cream until smooth, then stir in the butter, soaked raisins and rum. Pour into the dry ingredients and stir together until just mixed, then spoon large dollops of the mixture into the prepared muffin pan.

Bake for about 20 minutes until risen and golden. Leave to cool in the pan for a few minutes, then transfer to a wire rack to cool.

Cool and creamy carrot cake

If you fancy making a dairy-free version of these muffins, just use soya milk instead of regular milk, and omit the frosting. They're still fab served plain, warm from the oven with just a drizzle of honey on top.

✳ Makes 12

300 g/10 oz/2 cups self-raising flour
1 tsp baking powder
1 tsp ground cinnamon
75 g/2¾ oz/scant ¾ cup walnut pieces
115 g/4 oz/½ cup soft brown sugar
2 eggs, beaten
200 ml/7 fl oz/generous ¾ cup milk
150 ml/5 fl oz/scant ⅔ cup sunflower oil
1 large carrot, grated
finely grated zest of 1 orange

For the topping
150 g/5 oz cream cheese
50 g/1¾ oz/⅓ cup icing sugar, sifted
1 tsp lemon juice
12 walnut halves

Preheat the oven to 200°C/400°F/Gas 6. Grease or line a 12-hole muffin pan.

Combine the flour, baking powder and cinnamon and sift into a large bowl, then scatter the walnut pieces on top.

In a separate bowl, combine the brown sugar, eggs, milk and oil and beat lightly until well mixed, then stir in the grated carrot and orange zest. Pour into the dry ingredients and stir together until just combined, then spoon big dollops of the mixture into the prepared muffin pan.

Bake for about 20 minutes until risen and golden. Leave to cool in the pan for a few minutes, then transfer to a wire rack to cool completely.

To decorate, beat together the cream cheese, icing sugar and lemon juice until smooth and creamy. Swirl the frosting on top of the muffins and top each one with a walnut half.

Apricot and marzipan magic

Sweet, golden, meltingly tender and so, so easy to make, these fabulous almondy, fruity muffins are just divine. You can eat them any time, but I like them mid-afternoon with a nice cup of Earl Grey in the prettiest teacup I can find.

✳ Makes 12

300 g/10 oz/2 cups plain flour
1 tbsp baking powder
100 g/3½ oz/scant ½ cup caster sugar
85 g/3 oz marzipan, finely grated
2 eggs, beaten
175 ml/5½ fl oz/¾ cup milk
85 g/3 oz butter, melted
85 g/3 oz ready-to-eat dried apricots, chopped
icing sugar, to dust (optional)

Preheat the oven to 200°C/400°F/Gas 6. Grease or line a 12-hole muffin pan.

Combine the flour, baking powder and caster sugar and sift into a large bowl, then sprinkle the grated marzipan on top.

In a separate bowl or jug, combine the eggs, milk and butter, then stir in the apricots. Pour the mixture into the dry ingredients and stir together until just combined, then spoon large dollops of the mixture into the prepared muffin pan.

Bake for about 20 minutes until risen and golden, then leave to cool in the pan for a few minutes. Transfer to a wire rack to cool.

Serve dusted with icing sugar, if you like.

Black forest muffins

If you like the gateau, you'll absolutely love the muffins! These ones don't contain liqueur like the traditional cake does, but if you fancy a boozy twist, prick the tops of the muffins and drizzle a little kirsch over each one before decorating with whipped cream and cherries.

✱ Makes 12

100 g/3½ oz plain chocolate, chopped
85 g/3 oz butter
300 g/10 oz/2 cups plain flour
1 tbsp baking powder
150 g/5 oz/⅔ cup caster sugar
2 tbsp cocoa powder
200 g/7 oz/1½ cups black cherries, halved and pitted
200 ml/7 fl oz/generous ¾ cup milk
1 egg, beaten

To decorate
150 ml/5 fl oz/scant ⅔ cup double cream
12 black cherries
dark chocolate shavings

Preheat the oven to 200°C/400°F/Gas 6. Grease or line a 12-hole muffin pan.

Put the chocolate and butter in a heatproof bowl set over a pan of simmering water and leave until melted. Stir to combine, then set aside to cool.

Combine the flour, baking powder, sugar and cocoa and sift into a large bowl, then scatter the cherries on top.

Stir the milk and egg into the cooled chocolate mixture until smooth, then pour into the dry ingredients. Stir together until just mixed, then spoon big dollops of the mixture into the prepared muffin pan.

Bake for about 20 minutes until risen and just firm to the touch. Leave to cool in the pan for a few minutes, then transfer to a wire rack to cool completely.

To decorate, whip the cream until it stands in soft peaks, then spoon dollops on top of each muffin. Top with a cherry and decorate each one with a few chocolate shavings.

Savoury

4

Oh wonderful, wonderful savoury muffins! There are those days when you need a treat, but you just don't fancy something sugary – and this is where savoury muffins come into play. Cheesy ones, smoky ones, fishy ones, herby ones, seedy ones, spicy ones – so many options that sometimes it's difficult to work out which one to choose.

In terms of enjoyment, I utilise the same technique as I would with a sugary muffin. I sit down to relax, maybe with a glass of milk or juice, or even a glass of wine if it's getting to that time of day, and then I submerge myself totally in muffin heaven, letting my teeth sink into the warm, golden, crumbly crumb, and enjoying those salty, tangy, fragrant flavours as they make themselves known.

But that's just me – you can enjoy savoury muffins any way you like. They're great for breakfast – particularly breakfast on the run when you need to rush out of the house clutching a bit of brekkie in one hand and a briefcase in the other. But they're tops for lunchboxes and general daytime snacks, too – particularly if you're feeding kids and you're trying to restrict their consumption of sugar. And, better still, they make a wonderful addition to the lunch or dinner table – serve them as an accompaniment to soup or alongside a salad.

Crispy bacon muffins with chive butter

Go bonkers at breakfast and whip up a batch of these smoky bacon muffins as a treat! Enjoy them on the run or, for a lazy weekend, why not brew up a pot of coffee and enjoy with some scrambled eggs.

✳ Makes 12

6 tbsp olive oil
1 onion, finely chopped
8 rashers bacon, snipped into
    small pieces
300 g/10 oz/2 cups plain flour
1 tbsp baking powder
1 tbsp caster sugar
½ tsp salt
2 eggs, beaten
200 ml/7 fl oz/generous ¾ cup
    milk
3 tbsp chopped parsley
ground black pepper

For the chive butter
85 g/3 oz butter
2½ tbsp snipped chives
ground black pepper

To make the chive butter, beat the butter until soft, then mix in the chives and a good grinding of black pepper. Chill.

Preheat the oven to 200°C/400°F/Gas 6. Grease or line a 12-hole muffin pan.

Heat 2 tablespoons of the oil in a pan and gently fry the onion for 10 minutes until tender. Scoop out the onion on to a plate, then fry the bacon for a few minutes until cooked and crispy. Combine with the onion and set aside to cool.

Combine the flour, baking powder, sugar and salt and sift into a large bowl.

In a separate bowl, lightly beat the eggs, milk and remaining oil to combine, then stir in three-quarters of the onion and bacon and the parsley and a good grinding of black pepper. Pour the mixture into the dry ingredients and stir together until just combined. Spoon into the prepared muffin pan, sprinkle the remaining onion and bacon over the top, plus a good grinding of black pepper.

Bake for about 20 minutes until risen and golden brown. Leave to cool in the pan for a few minutes, then transfer to a wire rack. Serve warm with shavings of chive butter.

Spicy sweetcorn and jalapeño muffins

These sweet and spicy muffins have got a taste of the ol' south, where spicy, chilli-studded cornbread is all the rage. Eat them as they are, or break them open and serve with chunky guacamole, or avocado salsa, on top.

✴ Makes 12

150 g/5 oz/1 cup plain flour
150 g/5 oz/½ cup instant polenta
1 tbsp baking powder
½ tsp bicarbonate of soda
1 tbsp caster sugar
½ tsp salt
100 ml/3½ fl oz/scant ½ cup plain yogurt
75 ml/3 fl oz/scant ⅓ cup milk
2 tbsp sunflower oil
2 eggs, beaten
195 g/7 oz canned sweetcorn, drained
25 g/1 oz/3 tbsp bottled jalapeños, roughly chopped, plus extra to decorate

✴ You will find these pictured on p.77.

Preheat the oven to 200°C/400°F/Gas 6. Grease or line a 12-hole muffin pan.

Combine the flour, polenta, baking powder, bicarbonate of soda, sugar and salt and sift into a large bowl.

In a separate bowl, lightly beat the yogurt, milk, oil and eggs to combine, then stir in the sweetcorn and jalapeños. Pour into the dry ingredients and stir until just combined, then spoon dollops of the mixture into the prepared muffin pan.

Bake for about 20 minutes until well risen and golden brown. Leave to cool in the pan for a couple of minutes, then transfer to a wire rack to cool completely.

Cheese and onion muffins

There's a reason that cheese and onion are a classic combo –
and that's because they taste fantastic, particularly in these light,
herby muffins. Serve them warm for lunch or supper, take them on a
picnic – or grab one as a snack whenever you feel the need for a little
something to munch.

✳ Makes 12

6 tbsp olive oil
2 onions, finely chopped
300 g/10 oz/2 cups plain flour
1 tbsp baking powder
½ tsp salt
2 eggs, beaten
225 ml/8 fl oz/scant 1 cup milk
1 tsp fresh or dried thyme leaves
100 g/3½ oz mature Cheddar
    cheese, grated
ground black pepper

Preheat the oven to 200°C/400°F/Gas 6. Grease or line a
12-hole muffin pan.

Heat 2 tablespoons of the oil in a pan and gently fry the
onions for 10 minutes until tender. Set aside.

Combine the flour, baking powder and salt and sift into a
large bowl.

In a separate bowl, combine the eggs, milk, thyme and
remaining olive oil and add a good grinding of black pepper.
Stir in the onions and about three-quarters of the cheese,
then pour into the dry ingredients and mix together until
just combined. Spoon the mixture into the prepared muffin
pan and sprinkle with the remaining cheese and some
more black pepper.

Bake for about 20 minutes until well risen and golden.
Leave to cool in the pan for a minute, then transfer to a wire
rack to cool.

Four-seed pesto sensations

Scented with herby pesto and heaving with seeds, these yummy, wholesome-looking muffins are jam-packed with healthy oils to keep you fighting fit and bouncing bright. Serve them as an accompaniment to a meal, or pop one in your lunchbox.

✳ Makes 12

300 g/10 oz/2 cups plain flour
1 tbsp baking powder
1 tbsp caster sugar
½ tsp salt
2 tbsp sesame seeds
2 tbsp sunflower seeds
2 tbsp pumpkin seeds
2 tbsp poppy seeds
2 eggs, beaten
4 tbsp olive oil
3 tbsp pesto
175 ml/6 fl oz/¾ cup milk
ground black pepper

For the topping
2 tsp sesame seeds
2 tsp sunflower seeds
2 tsp pumpkin seeds
2 tsp poppy seeds

Preheat the oven to 200°C/400°F/Gas 6. Grease or line a 12-hole muffin pan.

Combine the seeds for the topping in a bowl and set aside.

Combine the flour, baking powder, sugar and salt and sift into a large bowl, then sprinkle the seeds over the top.

In a separate bowl or jug, lightly beat together the eggs, olive oil, pesto and milk and add a good grinding of black pepper. Pour into the dry ingredients and stir together until just combined. Spoon large dollops of the mixture into the prepared muffin pan, then sprinkle with the reserved topping seeds.

Bake for about 20 minutes until risen and golden. Leave to cool in the pan for a few minutes, then transfer to a wire rack to cool completely.

Sun-dried tomato and oregano muffins

Serve these yummy muffins warm or cold topped with sprigs of fresh oregano, and lose yourself in those rich Mediterranean flavours. For extra indulgence, split open a warm muffin and spread with herby cream cheese.

✳ Makes 12

300 g/10 oz/2 cups plain flour
1 tbsp baking powder
½ tsp salt
3 tbsp freshly grated Parmesan, plus extra for sprinkling
1 egg, beaten
250 ml/9 fl oz/1 cup milk
6 tbsp olive oil
6 sun-dried tomatoes, roughly chopped, plus 1 extra for sprinkling
1 garlic clove, finely chopped
1 tsp fresh oregano
ground black pepper

Preheat the oven to 190°C/375°F/Gas 5. Grease or line a 12-hole muffin pan.

Combine the flour, baking powder and salt and sift into a large bowl, then sprinkle the Parmesan into the bowl.

In a separate bowl, lightly beat together the egg, milk and oil to combine, then stir in the tomatoes, garlic and oregano. Add a good grinding of black pepper, then pour into the dry ingredients and stir until just combined. Spoon big dollops of the mixture into the prepared muffin pan and sprinkle Parmesan and a few pieces of sun-dried tomato over each one, then grind over more black pepper.

Bake for about 20 minutes until well risen and golden. Leave to cool in the pan for a couple of minutes, then transfer to a wire rack to cool completely.

Roast pepper and black olive muffins

Add a splash of Mediterranean colour to your muffin repertoire with these gorgeous cornmeal muffins. Chunks of sweet juicy pepper, shiny black olives and the bite of black pepper make these utterly moreish. They're faff-free, too, if you use bottled roasted peppers – although if you want to roast your own, why not?

✳ Makes 12

200 g/7 oz/1⅓ cups plain flour
100 g/3½ oz/⅔ cup cornmeal
1 tbsp baking powder
1 tbsp caster sugar
½ tsp salt
175 ml/6 fl oz/¾ cup buttermilk
2 eggs, beaten
85 g/3 oz butter, melted
4 large pieces of bottled roasted
    pepper, chopped (about
    125 g/4½ oz)
60 g/2 oz/½ cup pitted black
    olives, halved
ground black pepper

Preheat the oven to 200°C/400°F/Gas 6. Grease or line a 12-hole muffin pan.

Combine the flour, cornmeal, baking powder, sugar and salt and sift into a large bowl.

In a separate bowl, combine the buttermilk, eggs and butter with about two-thirds of the roasted peppers and olives, and add a good grinding of black pepper. Pour into the dry ingredients and stir together until just combined, then spoon big dollops of the mixture into the prepared muffin pan. Press the remaining roasted peppers and olives into the tops of the muffins and grind over more black pepper.

Bake for about 20 minutes until risen and golden. Leave to cool in the pan for a few minutes, then transfer to a wire rack to cool.

Ole south chilli cornmeal

These are the muffins to serve to your dairy-intolerant friends and family for breakfast, lunch or dinner. With a tender yellow crumb and sweet-spicy bite, they've got a taste of southern-style cornbread about them.

✳ Makes 12

115 g/4 oz/½ cup cornmeal
175 g/6 oz/¾ cup plain flour
1 tbsp baking powder
½ tsp salt
½ tsp crushed dried chilli, plus extra for sprinkling
1 egg, beaten
3 tbsp olive oil
175 ml/6 fl oz/¾ cup soya milk
½ green pepper, diced

Preheat the oven to 200°C/400°F/Gas 6. Grease or line a 12-hole muffin pan.

Combine the cornmeal, flour, baking powder and salt and sift into a large bowl. Sprinkle over the crushed chilli.

In a separate bowl, combine the egg, oil and soya milk, then stir in the diced pepper. Pour into the dry ingredients and stir together, then spoon big dollops of the mixture into the prepared muffin pan. Sprinkle over a little more dried chilli.

Bake for about 15 minutes until risen and firm. Leave to cool in the pan for a few minutes, then transfer to a wire rack to cool.

Smoked salmon sophistication

In all honesty, muffins probably aren't the most sophisticated baked treat known to mankind. But these ones made with smoked salmon and cream cheese are doing their level best to try! Try serving them as a quirky savoury for afternoon tea – something of a mix between smoked salmon sandwiches and freshly baked scones...

✳ Makes 12

300 g/10 oz/2 cups plain flour
1 tbsp baking powder
1 tbsp caster sugar
½ tsp salt
75 g/2¾ oz cream cheese, plus
    extra to serve
200 ml/7 fl oz/generous ¾ cup
    milk
1 large egg, beaten
60 g/2 oz butter, melted
100 g/3½ oz smoked salmon,
    snipped into small pieces
2 spring onions, chopped
1 tsp fresh dill, chopped
ground black pepper
fresh dill sprigs, to garnish

Preheat the oven to 200°C/400°F/Gas 6. Grease or line a 12-hole muffin pan.

Combine the flour, baking powder, sugar and salt and sift into a large bowl.

In a separate bowl, beat the cream cheese until soft, then gradually beat in the milk until smooth and creamy. Stir in the egg and butter, followed by the salmon, spring onions, dill and a good grinding of black pepper. Pour into the dry ingredients and stir until just combined, then spoon big dollops of the mixture into the prepared muffin pan and grind over a little more black pepper.

Bake for about 20 minutes until risen and golden. Leave to cool in the pan for a few minutes, then transfer to a wire rack to cool.

Serve spread with more cream cheese and fresh dill sprigs to decorate.

Fragrant courgette and parmesan

Tender and moist and packed with juicy shreds of courgette, these muffins are best eaten while still slightly warm from the oven. The combination of mild courgette, piquant capers, fragrant dill and salty Parmesan comes together to create a truly sublime muffin, puffed up and golden – and utterly irresistible!

✳ Makes 12

300 g/10 oz/2 cups plain flour
1 tbsp baking powder
1 tbsp caster sugar
½ tsp salt
1 egg, beaten
175 ml/6 fl oz/¾ cup milk
115 g/4 oz butter, melted
2 tbsp capers, roughly chopped
1 tsp dried dill
5 tbsp freshly grated Parmesan,
 plus extra for sprinkling
1 courgette, grated
ground black pepper

Preheat the oven to 200°C/400°F/Gas 6. Grease or line a 12-hole muffin pan.

Combine the flour, baking powder, sugar and salt and sift into a large bowl.

In a separate bowl, combine the egg, milk, melted butter, capers, dill, Parmesan and courgette and add a good grinding of black pepper. Pour the courgette mixture into the dry ingredients and quickly stir together until just combined. Spoon dollops of the mixture into the prepared muffin pan and sprinkle with a little more Parmesan and a little black pepper.

Bake for about 30 minutes until well risen and golden. Leave to cool in the pan for a few minutes, then transfer to a wire rack to cool. Eat warm or cold.

Tangy spinach and feta

Go Greek with this timeless combination of tender green spinach and salty, tangy feta. These muffins are fabulous for a brunch or buffet, and great thrown in a lunchbox or served alongside soup or salad. If you want to ring the changes, try adding a teaspoon of dried dill to the mixture, or throw in a couple of tablespoons of toasted pinenuts for a bit of texture.

✳ Makes 12

4 tbsp olive oil
1 garlic clove, finely chopped
200 g/7 oz spinach
300 g/10 oz/2 cups plain flour
pinch of salt
1 tbsp baking powder
2 tbsp caster sugar
pinch of dried crushed chilli
1 egg, beaten
275 ml/9½ fl oz/generous 1 cup
  milk
115 g/4 oz feta cheese, crumbled
2 spring onions, chopped

Preheat the oven to 200°C/400°F/Gas 6. Grease or line a 12-hole muffin pan.

Heat half the oil in a large pan and fry the garlic for about 1 minute. Add the spinach and sauté for a couple of minutes until wilted and tender. Leave to cool, then squeeze out any excess liquid and chop.

Combine the flour, salt, baking powder and sugar and sift into a large bowl, then sprinkle the crushed chilli over the top.

In a separate bowl, lightly beat together the egg, milk and remaining oil to combine, then stir in the feta, spinach and spring onions. Pour into the dry ingredients and stir together until just combined, then spoon the mixture into the prepared muffin pan.

Bake for about 20 minutes until risen and golden. Leave to cool in the pan for a couple of minutes, then transfer to a wire rack to cool completely.

Seasonal

5

The wonderful thing about muffins is that they're great at any time, for any occasion – but what's even better is that they're perfectly suited to all those special occasions as well. Christmas? Easter? Valentine's Day? Birthday? Hallowe'en? No problem – there's a muffin just begging to be baked!

Celebrate in style with specially designed and dedicated muffins – whether they're sparkling for Bastille Day, glowing with birthday candles, or just prettier than pretty for Mother's Day. These muffins don't have to fulfil the old clichés of a Christmas or simnel cake – they might take their inspiration from tradition, but they offer a whole new twist on the old-fashioned favourites to create magical, mystical celebration extravaganzas!

Another bonus of baking a batch of special seasonal muffins is that they're just perfect for turning into a gift. Arrange them in a pretty box or basket, snuggling them down into a nest of crumpled tissue paper, then watch their recipient's face light up with excitement when you present your gift to them. After all, wouldn't a batch of specially baked muffins make anyone's day?

Easter muffins

When you're celebrating Easter with a gluten- or dairy-intolerant muffin-eater, this is the recipe to choose. Inspired by the fruity marzipan simnel cake, these little muffins look cuter than cute topped off with baby chick yellow frosting and pastel-coloured eggs. Be sure to check the ingredients on your pastel-coloured eggs and marzipan to make sure they don't contain any dairy or gluten.

✳ Makes 12

200 g/7 oz/1⅓ cups potato flour
100 g/3½ oz/⅔ cup rice flour
1 tbsp cornflour
1 tbsp gluten-free baking powder
100 g/3½ oz/scant ½ cup caster sugar
100 g/3½ oz/⅔ cup raisins or sultanas
2 tbsp candied peel
1 egg, beaten
175 ml/6 fl oz/¾ cup soya milk
6 tbsp sunflower oil
100 g/3½ oz gluten-free marzipan, finely grated
finely grated zest of 1 lemon

To decorate
200 g/7 oz/1¾ cup icing sugar, sifted
2 tbsp lemon juice
yellow food colouring
pastel-coloured mini eggs

Preheat the oven to 200°C/400°F/Gas 6. Grease or line a 12-hole muffin pan.

Combine the flours, baking powder and caster sugar and sift into a large bowl, then add the raisins or sultanas and candied peel.

In a separate bowl or jug, combine the egg, milk and oil, then stir in the marzipan and lemon zest. Pour into the dry ingredients and stir together until just combined, then spoon large dollops of the mixture into the prepared muffin pan.

Bake for about 20 minutes until risen and golden. Leave to cool in the pan for a few minutes, then transfer to a wire rack to cool.

To decorate, mix the icing sugar and lemon juice until smooth, then add a few drops of food colouring to make a pale yellow frosting. Spoon on top of the cakes and top with mini eggs.

Spring flower favourites

Bake these creamy, lemony muffins scented with cardamom just because it's spring and the sun's shining. Or, if you're the caring, sharing type, why not whip up a batch for mum on Mother's Day?

✳ Makes 12

300 g/10 oz/2 cups plain flour
1 tbsp baking powder
150 g/5 oz/⅔ cup caster sugar
1 egg, beaten
225 ml/8 fl oz/scant 1 cup milk
grated zest of 1 lemon
seeds from 6 cardamom pods,
    crushed
85 g/3 oz butter, melted
sugar spring flowers, to decorate

For the frosting
150 g/5 oz mascarpone
3 tbsp icing sugar, sifted
1½ tsp lemon juice
yellow food colouring

✳ You will find these pictured
    on p.95.

Preheat the oven to 200°C/400°F/Gas 6. Grease or line a 12-hole muffin pan.

Combine the flour, baking powder and caster sugar and sift into a large bowl.

In a separate bowl or jug, combine the egg and milk, then stir in the lemon zest, cardamom seeds and butter. Pour into the dry ingredients and stir together until just combined, then spoon large dollops of the mixture into the prepared muffin pan.

Bake for 20 minutes until risen and golden. Leave to cool in the pan for a few minutes, then transfer to a wire rack to cool.

To decorate, beat together the mascarpone, icing sugar and lemon juice until smooth and creamy, then add a few drops of yellow colouring to make a pretty buttercup yellow. Swirl on top of the muffins and decorate with sugar spring flowers.

Summer berry fruities

Go on and indulge yourself with all that glorious summer fruit. Take your pick from what's in season – whether it's a simple combination such as strawberry and blueberry, or a full-on summer extravanganza with strawberries, raspberries, redcurrants, blueberries and cherries! I've suggested topping these golden treats with an indulgent cream cheese frosting – but they're just as good served plain.

✱ Makes 12

175 g/6 oz/1⅔ cup summer
   berries, such as strawberries,
   blueberries, raspberries
   and/or pitted cherries
300 g/10 oz/2 cups self-raising
   flour
1 tsp baking powder
150 g/5 oz/⅔ cup caster sugar
100 ml/3½ fl oz/scant ½ cup
   plain yogurt
125 ml/4 fl oz/½ cup milk
1 egg, lightly beaten
1 tsp vanilla essence
125 g/4½ oz butter, melted

For the frosting
150 g/5 oz cream cheese
50 g/1¾ oz/⅓ cup icing sugar
2 tsp lemon juice
fresh summer berries, to
   decorate

Preheat the oven to 200°C/400°F/Gas 6. Line a 12-hole muffin pan with paper cases. Cut larger berries, such as strawberries, into blueberry-sized pieces.

Combine the flour, baking powder and caster sugar and sift together into a large bowl, then scatter about three-quarters of the berries on top.

In a separate bowl or jug, stir together the yogurt, milk, egg, vanilla and butter, then pour into the dry ingredients and stir roughly until just combined. Spoon dollops of the mixture into the muffin cases and sprinkle the remaining berries on top, pressing down slightly.

Bake for about 20 minutes until risen and golden. Leave to cool in the pan for a few minutes, then transfer to a wire rack to cool completely.

To decorate, beat together the cream cheese, icing sugar and lemon juice and swirl on top of the muffins, then top with fresh berries.

Redcurrant love hearts

With a swirled cheesecake topping on these muffins, they're hard to resist. So go on – bake up a batch for the love of your life and wow them with your baking skills! After all, how could they resist you after that...?

♥ Makes 12

300 g/10 oz/2 cups self-raising
   flour
1 tsp baking powder
150 g/5 oz/⅔ cup caster sugar
100 g/3½ oz redcurrants, plus
   extra to decorate
225 ml/8 fl oz/scant 1 cup milk
1 egg, beaten
85 g/3 oz butter, melted
1 tsp vanilla essence

For the filling
150 g/5 oz cream cheese
150 g/5 oz/⅔ cup caster sugar
1 egg, beaten
¼ tsp vanilla essence

Preheat the oven to 200°C/400°F/Gas 6. Line a 12-hole heart-shaped muffin pan with heart-shaped papers.

First make the filling. Beat together the cream cheese and sugar until creamy, then beat in the egg and vanilla until smooth and creamy. Set aside.

To make the muffins, combine the flour, baking powder and sugar and sift together into a large bowl. Strip the currants from their stems and add the fruit to the flour.

In a separate bowl or jug, combine the milk, egg, butter and vanilla, then pour over the dry ingredients. Gently stir together until just combined, then spoon big dollops of the mixture into the paper cases. Top each one with a dollop of the cream cheese mixture, swirling it into the muffin mixture.

Bake for about 20 minutes until risen and golden. Leave to cool in the pan for a few minutes, then transfer to a wire rack to cool.

To serve, top each muffin with a sprig of redcurrants.

Hallowe'en super scaries

It's the time of year to roast some squash or pumpkin and then throw it into these irresistibly sweet and spicy muffins. Look out for fake spiders and other nasties in kids' toy shops and hide a few on the plate to scare anyone else away ... leaving you with a big batch of muffins all to yourself!

✳ Makes 12

200 g/7 oz peeled, seeded
  butternut squash or pumpkin,
  cut into chunks
½ tbsp sunflower oil
300 g/10 oz/2 cups plain flour
1 tbsp baking powder
1 tsp ground cinnamon
1 egg, beaten
150 ml/5 fl oz/scant ⅔ cup
  soured cream
50 ml/1¾ fl oz milk
115 g/4 oz/½ cup soft brown
  sugar
60 g/2 oz butter, melted

To decorate
150 g/5 oz white chocolate
25 g/1 oz dark chocolate

Preheat the oven to 190°C/375°F/Gas 5. Put the squash in a baking dish, drizzle with the oil, then toss to coat. Roast for about 35 minutes until tender. Remove from the oven and leave to cool, then mash roughly with a fork.

To make the muffins, preheat the oven to 200°C/400°F/ Gas 6. Grease or line a 12-hole muffin pan.

Combine the flour, baking powder and cinnamon and sift into a large bowl.

In a separate bowl, combine the egg, soured cream, milk, mashed squash, sugar and butter and stir together until well mixed. Pour into the dry ingredients and stir together until just combined, then spoon large dollops of the mixture into the prepared muffin pan.

Bake for about 20 minutes until risen and golden. Leave to cool in the pan for a few minutes, then transfer to a wire rack.

To decorate, melt the white chocolate in a heatproof bowl set over a pan of barely simmering water, then spoon on top of the cakes. Melt the dark chocolate in the same way in a separate bowl, then spoon into a piping bag with a very narrow nozzle. Pipe concentric circles on to each cake, then use a skewer to draw a line from the centre to the outside of each cake to make a spider's web pattern.

Fabulous fireworks

Bang! Pop! Whizz! Whether it's firework night, Bastille Day or the Fourth of July – bake up a batch of these muffin sparklers to get with the firework theme! You could go for the tasteful all-silver sparkler look, but personally I like them covered in utterly over-the-top coloured sparkling balls and stars.

✳ Makes 12

250 g/9 oz/1⅔ cup self-raising flour
1 tsp baking powder
150 g/5 oz/⅔ cup caster sugar
3 tbsp cocoa powder
4 tbsp ground almonds
2 eggs, beaten
175 ml/6 fl oz/¾ cup milk
100 g/3½ oz butter, melted

To decorate
25 g/1 oz butter
1½ tbsp cocoa powder
2 tbsp boiling water
150 g/5 oz/1⅓ cup icing sugar, sifted
tiny edible silver or coloured shiny balls and stars, for sprinkling
12 mini indoor sparklers

Preheat the oven to 200°C/400°F/Gas 6. Grease or line a 12-hole muffin pan.

Combine the flour, baking powder, sugar and cocoa and sift into a large bowl, then sprinkle the almonds into the bowl.

In a separate bowl or jug, combine the eggs, milk and butter, then pour into the dry ingredients. Stir together until combined, then spoon large dollops of the mixture into the prepared muffin pan.

Bake for about 20 minutes until risen and firm to the touch. Leave to cool in the pan for a couple of minutes, then transfer to a wire rack to cool.

To decorate, put the butter in a heatproof bowl set over a pan of simmering water and leave to melt. Stir in the cocoa until smooth, then stir in the boiling water. Gradually stir in the icing sugar and stir for about 2 minutes until glossy – if very thick, stir in a drop more water. Spoon over the muffins, then sprinkle with shiny balls and stars and stick a sparkler in the centre of each one.

Pear and cranberry muffins

Get festive and enjoy a white Christmas with these snow-topped
Christmas muffins. Have everything measured out on Christmas Eve
so you can whip them together and throw them in the oven in time for
tearing into your stocking full of goodies the next morning!

✳ Makes 12

300 g/10 oz/2 cups self-raising
   flour
½ tsp bicarbonate of soda
150 g/5 oz/⅔ cup caster sugar
½ tsp mixed spice
2 eggs, beaten
100 ml/3½ fl oz/scant ½ cup
   plain yogurt
75 ml/2½ fl oz/scant ⅓ cup milk
100 g/3½ oz butter, melted
2 pears, peeled, cored and diced
60 g/2 oz/⅓ cup dried
   cranberries

To decorate
150 g/5 oz mascarpone
3 tbsp icing sugar, sifted
36 fresh cranberries
12 small holly leaves

Preheat the oven to 200°C/400°F/Gas 6. Grease or line a
12-hole muffin pan.

Combine the flour, bicarbonate of soda, caster sugar and
mixed spice and sift into a large bowl.

In a separate bowl, combine the eggs, yogurt, milk and
butter. Stir in the pears and cranberries, then pour into the
dry ingredients and stir together until just combined. Spoon
large dollops of the mixture into the prepared muffin pan.

Bake for about 20 minutes until risen and golden. Leave to
cool in the pan for a few minutes, then transfer to a wire
rack to cool.

To decorate, beat together the mascarpone and icing sugar
and swirl on top of each cooled muffin, then arrange three
cranberries and a holly leaf on top of each one.

Mince pie magic

Get in the festive spirit with these light and fluffy muffin mince pies –
so much better than the pastry original. Break open the lightly spiced
citrus crumb with a tang of Grand Marnier and find lashings of
moreish mincemeat hidden inside. Serve them warm – just as they are
– or for an indulgent dessert try them with brandy sauce poured over...

✳ Makes 12

300 g/10 oz/2 cups plain flour
1 tbsp baking powder
115 g/4 oz/½ cup caster sugar
½ tsp ground ginger
¼ tsp freshly grated nutmeg
175 ml/6 fl oz/¾ cup milk
2 tbsp Grand Marnier
1 egg, beaten
115 g/4 oz butter, melted
finely grated zest of 1 lemon
about 6 tbsp luxury mincemeat
icing sugar and silver edible
    glitter, for dusting
holly leaves, to decorate

Preheat the oven to 200°C/400°F/Gas 6. Grease or line a
12-hole muffin pan.

Combine the flour, baking powder, caster sugar, ginger and
nutmeg and sift into a large bowl.

In a separate bowl or jug, combine the milk, Grand Marnier,
egg, butter and lemon zest. Pour into the dry ingredients
and stir together until just combined. Half fill each muffin
cup with the mixture, top with a heaped teaspoon of
mincemeat, nestling it down into the mixture, then top with
another dollop of muffin mixture to cover.

Bake for about 20 minutes until risen and golden. Leave to
cool in the pan for a few minutes, then transfer to a wire
rack to cool.

To serve, dust with icing sugar, decorate with a holly leaf
and sprinkle with a little silver glitter.

Index

Page numbers in **bold** denote
an illustration

almonds
lemon and almond crumbles
24, 25
apple muffins with cinnamon
butter **18**, 19
apricot and marzipan magic **72**, 73

bacon
crispy bacon muffins with
chive butter **78**, 79
bananas
banoffee toffees 62
nutty banana and choc chip
chomps 20
banoffee toffees 62
beetroot bonanza **40**, 41
berries
summer berry fruities 99
birthday mini muffins 50, **50**
black forest muffins 74, **75**
blueberry bliss **15**, 21

cardamom
spring flower favourites 98
carrots
cool and creamy carrot cake 71
cheese
fragrant courgette and
Parmesan muffins 92
and onion muffins 81
tangy spinach and feta
muffins 93
cherries
black forest muffins 74, **75**
white chocolate, cherry and
macadamia muffins 64, **65**
chillies
ole south chilli cornmeal
muffins **88**, 89

spicy sweetcorn and jalapeño
muffins **77**, 80
chives
crispy bacon muffins with
chive butter **78**, 79
chocolate
birthday mini muffins 50, **50**
black forest muffins 74, **75**
espresso express 60, **61**
hazelnut melts **66**, 67
nutty banana and choc chip
chomps 20
peanut butter and choc chip
cheekies 36, **37**
rocky roadsters 52, **53**
triple choc-chunkies **59**, 63
white chocolate, cherry and
macadamia muffins 64, **65**
Christmas muffins 106, **107**
cinnamon
apple muffins with cinnamon
butter **18**, 19
coconut-lime muffins 16, **17**
coffee
espresso express 60, **61**
coloured candies 42, **43**
cornmeal
ole south chilli cornmeal
muffins **88**, 89
roast pepper and black olive
muffins 86, **87**
courgettes
fragrant courgette and
Parmesan muffins 92
cranberries
pear and cranberry muffins
106, **107**
cream cheese
redcurrant love hearts
100, **101**
smoked salmon sophistication
90, **91**

crispy bacon muffins with
chive butter **78**, 79
custard
tangy rhubarb and custard
muffins **28**, 29

date and ginger honeys 26, **27**
donuts, jammy **34**, 35

Easter muffins 96, **97**
espresso express 60, **61**

fabulous fireworks **104**, 105
feta cheese
tangy spinach and feta
muffins 93
figgy oatmeal muffins 51
firework muffins **104**, 105
four-seed pesto sensations 82, **83**
fragrant courgette and Parmesan
muffins 92
fudge
vanilla fudgies 46

ginger
date and ginger honeys 26, **27**

Hallowe'en super scaries 102, **103**
hazelnuts
chocolate hazelnut melts **66**, 67
honey
date and ginger honeys 26, **27**
honey-nut muffins 47

jammy donuts **34**, 35

lemon(s)
and almond crumbles **24**, 25
luscious lemon and raspberry
muffins 68, **69**
spring flower favourites 98
limes
coconut-lime muffins 16, **17**

M&Ms
  coloured candies 42, **43**
macadamia nuts
  white chocolate, cherry and
  macadamia muffins 64, **65**
mangos
  tropical temptations 54, **55**
maple syrup
  spiced maple and pecan
  munchies 22, **23**
marshmallows
  rocky roadsters 52, **53**
marzipan
  apricot and marzipan magic
  72, 73
  Easter muffins 96, **97**
mince pie magic **108**, 109
mini fruit marvels 38, **39**
mints
  peppermint stick muffins 48, **49**
muesli morning muffins 30

nuts
  chocolate hazelnut melts **66**, 67
  honey-nut muffins 47
  lemon and almond crumbles
  24, 25
  nutty banana and choc chip
  chomps 20
  rocky roadsters 52, **53**
  spiced maple and pecan
  munchies 22, **23**
  white chocolate, cherry and
  macadamia muffins 64, **65**
Nutella
  chocolate hazelnut melts **66**, 67
  nutty banana and choc chip
  chomps 20

oats
  figgy oatmeal muffins 51
ole south chilli cornmeal muffins
  88, 89
olives
  roast pepper and black olive
  muffins 86, **87**

onions
  cheese and onion muffins 81
oranges
  spotty dotty orange and poppy
  seed muffins 31
oregano
  sun-dried tomato and oregano
  muffins **84**, 85

Parmesan
  fragrant courgette and
  Parmesan muffins 92
peanut butter and choc chip
  cheekies 36, **37**
pear and cranberry muffins
  106, **107**
pecan nuts
  spiced maple and pecan
  munchies 22, **23**
peppermint stick muffins 48, **49**
peppers
  roast pepper and black olive
  muffins 86, **87**
pesto
  four-seed pesto sensations 82, **83**
pineapple
  tropical temptations 54, **55**
poppy seeds
  spotty dotty orange and poppy
  seed muffins 31
pumpkin
  Hallowe'en super scaries 102, **103**

raisins
  min fruit marvels 38, **39**
  rum-raisin muffins 70
raspberries
  luscious lemon and raspberry
  muffins 68, **69**
redcurrant love hearts 100, **101**
rhubarb
  tangy rhubarb and custard
  muffins **28**, 29
roast pepper and black olive
  muffins 86, **87**
rocky roadsters 52, **53**

rum-raisin muffins 70

seeds
  four-seed pesto sensations
  82, **83**
  muesli morning muffins 30
smarties
  coloured candies 42, **43**
smoked salmon sophistication
  90, **91**
spiced maple and pecan
  munchies 22, **23**
spicy sweetcorn and jalapeño
  muffins **77**, 80
spinach
  tangy spinach and feta
  muffins 93
spotty dotty orange and
  poppy seed muffins 31
spring flower favourites **95**, 98
squash
  Hallowe'en super scaries
  102, **103**
summer berry fruities 99
sun-dried tomato and oregano
  muffins **84**, 85
sweetcorn
  spicy sweetcorn and jalapeño
  muffins **77**, 80

tangy rhubarb and custard
  muffins **28**, 29
tangy spinach and feta
  muffins 93
tomatoes
  sun-dried tomato and oregano
  muffins **84**, 85
triple choc-chunkies **59**, 63
tropical temptations 54, **55**

vanilla fudgies 46

white chocolate
  cherry and macadamia
  muffins 64, **65**

Acknowledgements

Thanks go to all my tasters – but especially to David, for so willingly piling on the pounds in the face of muffin madness.

Publisher's acknowledgements: Thanks to our models, Rhys and Florence, for having so much fun! Thanks also to cakeadoodledo.co.uk and Charlotte Barton for allowing us to use the photograph on page 12. And to Jane Howorth at the Battery Hen Welfare Trust.